Tailored Dreams

~By~
Daniel Christian Bradley

Christ Communications Publishing

Tailored Dreams

[tey-ler-ed dreems]

A vision of a predestined outcome designed by God for a specific person and a specific time.

Aligning one's lifestyle to fit the God ordained purpose for their life, living spiritually tailored.

Tailored Dreams

By
Daniel Christian Bradley

Library of Congress Cataloging-in-Publication Data
ISBN 978-0-692-76875-4

Printed in the United States of America

Dedication

I dedicate this book to my wife, Shekha Bradley, for challenging me to be a better man each day and holding me accountable to living a full life; my mother Angela Bradley for raising me to be the tailored dreamer I am today, and to all of the young people I have had the pleasure to work with over the years, who have taught me as much as I have tried to impart to them.

And to my spiritual mentors, Rev. Tony Lee and Rev. Bill Lee of Community of Hope AME Church, thank you for teaching me that I serve a God big enough to grant me enough grace for my future and mercy for my past. I am embracing the "shift," and I am 10 times better.

Acknowledgments

I would like to acknowledge my family, all of my aunts, uncles, cousins and close friends. Your relationships have helped me through so many trials and your advice has inspired much of this book.

This process could not have been successful without Editor Frank Dexter Brown and Natasha T. Brown of Brown & Duncan Brand.

Contents

foreword
by Shekha Bradley

Just like the stripes on a zebra, and our uniquely intricate fingerprints, God has destined for each of us an exclusively tailored purpose and dream to fulfill on earth. It is imperative to focus solely on YOUR unique purpose and not continuously compare yourself to others. It's so easy to get caught up watching others, striving for the dreams we "think" we should have and coveting the rewards of other people's callings. Although it is important to "sharpen the iron" of your friends and keep successful people in your inner circle, be wary of a constant comparison of your life to those you know. It can be detrimental to hitting your target in life. God has designed only ONE you, and therefore only YOU can fulfill your infinitely unique purpose on this earth. What you were put here to do—NO ONE ELSE can ever do. Isn't that amazing? No person that came before you and no person that comes after you will be doing the exact thing that God called YOU to do. I think that's crazy good and it makes me feel empowered and excited to do "my thing" in this world. Your mind, your skills, your passion, your heart, your personality, your character, your temperament, your morals, your values, your

1

thought processes and everything in between are what makes you, YOU.

Before I met Daniel, I was an extremely accomplished young scholar, having graduated from the Science and Technology program at Oxon Hill High School, flourishing in my college career at Howard University by being extremely active on campus and obtaining my Bachelor's of Science there. I was working at a world renowned research company and had already been accepted and making plans to attend the Harvard University Graduate School of Education, just weeks before Daniel and I were introduced. I really thought I had a great handle on setting and achieving my dreams. However, I hadn't made the connections between my gifts, talents, goals, dreams and purpose in life. Although these accomplishments were purposed and divinely orchestrated by God, they felt like generic, "cookie cutter" dreams—be successful, graduate from school, go to grad school, get married, have children, grow in my career, etc. It's as if I was completing things and gathering puzzle pieces to success, I just hadn't really started putting them together to form my destiny. And along came Daniel, the charming and beautiful dream coach who happened to really like me. ☺

After having intimate conversations with Daniel, and allowing his gifts to flourish within my life, I have truly transformed my way of thinking and the confidence I have in my specific God-given talents. I have stopped competing with others (so much) and discovered a new-found peace about the track my life is on. It's my lane, all by myself and only I can complete the missions purposed for me along the way. My life has become much more driven, more specifically geared to individualized targets in life. I want precise results from my family, from myself and from all people I may impact.

Daniel and I have only been together five years (married seven months, at the time of this writing) and in that short time, I noticed that he has a "gift" for fostering a person's dedication and confidence to live out their unique purpose on this earth. I believe in my heart, with everything I have, that Daniel's mission and God-given purpose is to help others achieve their dreams. I've watched Daniel fight his own personal storms while simultaneously encouraging others and motivating them out of their turmoil. It's truly inspiring to watch him allow God to work through him, for others. I encourage you to read this book, take notes, pray and meditate on the lessons and apply them to your life. Allow Daniel to help you tailor your dreams, along with the discernment from God, and begin to put all of your puzzle pieces together. Your unique purpose and God-given mission is still out there, waiting for you to come and achieve it!

Daniel, I am proud to be your wife, and truly excited about the vision God has given you for our lives. You make my heart full and I am SUPER excited to be along for this awesome ride!...**I can rightly say I knew you when** ;-)

All my love,
Your Wife!

Tailored Dreams

one
Conversation with a Dreamer

Dear Young Dreamer,

As you embark on this journey of becoming an adult, you'll receive literally tons of advice. Most of it you'll ignore, as I did at your age, because after all, who knows what you need better than you do? At least that's how I thought as a teenager. I still remember my first day of classes in college. I sat in a classroom on that fall morning not knowing that I was in what I now know was one of the most defining moments of my life. I was a student at Prince George's Community College and my first class was African American Studies. The professor, whose name I can't recall, taught a lesson that day that I've never forgotten. He had a question written on the board: Are you a laborer or a thinker?

That question has played in my mind throughout my adult life. Basically, it suggests that you can support yourself through physical labor or by getting paid as intellectual property. I learned quickly that I wanted to be a thinker. I wanted to do something that would greatly impact the world. The real question was how? How would I go about becoming what I wanted to be when I grew up?

After years of trial and error, I remembered the words of a quote I heard once: "Measure twice, cut once," which basically means spend more time thinking before you act. To me, it meant to become calculating. I've learned that no one has ever become successful by accident, or for that matter, no one has failed by accident, either. Your future is not determined by fate. It's achieved through faith, through an undying will to succeed, and through a strongly defined work ethic— yes, no matter what, you still have to do the work. You still have to formulate a well-laid plan and then be auda- cious enough to actually enact it. The classes you take, the lessons learned from listening to wise counsel, or even from making the wrong decision, is where you begin to form that plan—the study sessions, scholarly debates in class, sessions with your mentors, advisors, parents, and even peers all are ingredients to the plan you will one day have to create.

My college years did two things for me: helped expand my worldview and helped to build my network. They also taught me, by default, that I didn't know everything. During those years I thought I had a perfect plan, and at that time, my plan didn't include staying in college. I soon left, believing not just the lie I told myself. I would say, "What's the point? I can get more money without a degree." I believed another lie that has since gained popularity: That "college isn't for everybody." That's only a partially true statement. I learned later that the more complete version of that statement should be: "Every college isn't for everybody, but there is a place of higher education that's perfectly fit for you." I don't care whether you don't get the best grades, or feel like you hate school, there is a college, major and discipline for you. It may be a community college or a technical school, but for almost all of us there is a destination for continuing education post high school.

Dreaming Out Loud;Pursuing Process

There is a song that I love to listen to for motivation. It's called, "A Dream," it's by Shawn Corey Carter (Jay Z), the hip-hop artist, record producer and entrepreneur, and it says something else that is key for you to understand on your quest towards success: "Nobody [is] built like you, you design yourself." Think about it; let it sink in…*Nobody is built like you, you design yourself…*

There is no one in this world equipped to be you except you. If that's true than no two of us should have the exact same dream. We may be similar, we may be able to relate to each other, but no dream is one size fits all. You can become famous impersonating people, but you can only be successful, really great, or truly legendary, by being yourself. Your dreams are meant to be tailor made. They are meant to scare you at first, and maybe even make some people question your sanity. Your "Tailored Made Dreams" are driven by your "why"; your why is the reason behind what you do. For me, I wake up every day knowing it is my purpose to be a contributing architect of the future by encouraging, motivating, and inspiring young people. My why comes from the things that I have looked at in life and asked myself why is this thing this way? Former U.S. Senator Robert Francis "Bobby" Kennedy, who was assassinated in 1968 as he ran for the Democratic Party presidential nomination, said, "Some men see the world and say, why; dreamers look at the world and say, why not?"

I have always been the type of person who needed something to chase. I really think I enjoy "becoming," more than I do "being." Yes, I love the process. From the first passing thought, to finally having the resolve to say your dream out loud, to persevering through every opportunity to quit, and finally, that moment when you realize that the day you've been waiting for happened or is happening. I even love the private pep talks you give yourself in order to muster that 30 seconds of courage it takes to talk yourself back into your dream. I realized something at a very early age that most people never truly grasp: Nothing is impossible if you believe. History was by far my favorite subject in school, mostly because my textbooks were filled with stories of people who were thought initially to be fools or naively optimistic, but are remembered for accomplishing the things that conventional knowledge of the day said were impossible. One of the major prerequisites for pursuing dreams is to never be usual, conventional, or even normal.

The list goes on, starting with a caveman who dreamed of warmth, and then produced fire, to the Wright Brothers, who said long before R. Kelly, the phrase "I Believe I Can Fly," Henry Ford and his use of the first assembly line, George Washington Carver and his ability to show us how to cultivate peanuts and use

them thousands of ways (and who was the one who orig-
inated and developed the assembly-line idea for Ford).
The thing that all of those figures in the history books
had in common was that they all believed in their
abilities. And oddly enough what sounded crazy in one
generation is common in another. Did you ever think
about what Alexander Graham Bell's friends must have
thought when he tried to explain the idea of the
telephone to them? He literally was proposing inventing
a way to talk to people who were miles apart to a
generation whose best method of communication over
any distance was a letter. Perhaps the most important
dreamers were the founding fathers of the United States.
For instance, James Truslow Adams, who wrote of the
ideas and ideals of our great country and coined the
American Ethos "life, liberty and the pursuit of
happiness." Adams spoke of pursuing what we call the
"American Dream," which can be summed up as having
the opportunity to achieve as much in life as
determination, hard work, and ability will allow. It's
living in a country where we are all born free—though
few of us are born equal, we are at least free to "pursue."
In order to properly pursue your dreams you must tailor
them; you must fall in love with the "process."

Understanding that there are steps, a progression, that
no good thing in life just happens, but that most things
follow a very specific process—we want it, we want it
more, we dream it, we speak it—is part of what we must
learn. At the point that we've said it out loud is usually
your first turning point because our own self-doubt can
be our dream's worst enemy. You can use the information
and skills you learn in class to give confidence to your

dream. Take the classes that will challenge you, that will force you to stretch your mind. Don't be afraid of failing; instead fear quitting. Quitting is the assassination of your dreams. So what if your dream seems impossible right now—with education, ambition, resilience, and a well-laid plan, anything is possible.

Designing Yourself: Faith, Ambition and Painting Skies Blue

You see, we are all miracles. And what are miracles but impossible dreams? We were all born through process—a million sperm and only one egg, and the sperm that contained the specific genetic code needed to create us fertilized that one egg. For nine months, we developed safely in the womb, growing more each day, awaiting the painful, but rewarding moment of our birth when we became human. As we age, we get to recreate that miracle in numerous ways, and every time we make a dream, comes a new reality. We birth something into the world that did not exist before, just as our parents did with us. Out of the millions of ideas we had, that one made it and became fertile in our mind and grew as we worked for it. It takes shape as we get closer to its realization, and though there is no dream realized without some pain, it's all worth it once we *see* what at one point only existed in our mind's eye.

Adolescence is basically like a learner's permit for adulthood. It's supposed to be one of the few times in life when you're allowed to make some decisions (even mistakes), but hopefully under the instructive supervision of a wise parent, teacher, or mentor. Consider your teen years a part of your birthing process. The classes, the lessons, lectures; hanging out with friends, your first love, heartbreaks; learning to drive, studying for mid-terms and finals—all are necessary for the birthing of a healthy dream. So ask yourself: What am I here to contribute? Some of us will be like Steve Jobs and provide inventions that completely change multiple industries. Others of us will develop philosophy, art, or poetry that inspires future artists or philosophers. Some of us may simply be someone's "blue sky," meaning you are the happy place for people—you take pride in painting skies blue and helping to encourage others.

Whatever your answer to the question of your contribution (and that answer may change from time to time), use that assessment as your measuring tape as you utilize your education and integrity as the fabric for the tailoring of your dream, use failures as chalk to create the pattern you will need to guide your hand as you begin to cut out your dream, and then use your faith as the thread, and your ambition as the needle to sew it all together.

Henry David Thoreau, the great writer, poet and philosopher said, "If one advances confidently in the direction of his dreams, and endeavors to live the life which he has imagined, he will meet with a success unexpected in common hours." And in the time when that success seems so far away, and feels more and more unexpected, when it seems like all of your peers are succeeding and you feel stuck, remember that no dream is one size fits all. This is your path; don't measure your success by someone else's design. As Jay Z said,

"Remind yourself—nobody's built like you. You design yourself."

Remember young dreamer: You are young enough to try to be everything great. You will miss 100 percent of the dreams you choose not to chase, but what if you try one and make it? What if you become all you were meant to be? Yes, you can do that, young dreamer. Continue each night to dream the life you want, then wake up and live your dreams.

Sincerely,

Slightly Older Dreamer

two
Making of a Dream Maker

"Jacob lived in the land where his father had stayed, the land of Canaan. This is the account of Jacob's family line. Joseph, a young man of seventeen, was tending the flocks with his brothers, the sons of Bilhah and the sons of Zilpah, his father's wives, and he brought their father a bad report about them. Now Israel loved Joseph more than any of his other sons, because he had been born to him in his old age; and he made an ornate robe for him. When his brothers saw that their father loved him more than any of them, they hated him and could not speak a kind word to him. Joseph had a dream, and when he told it to his brothers, they hated him all the more. He said to them, 'Listen to this dream I had: We were binding sheaves of grain out in the field when suddenly my sheaf rose and stood upright, while your sheaves gathered around mine and bowed down to it.' His brothers said to him, 'Do you intend to reign over us? Will you actually rule us?' And they hated him all the more because of his dream and what he had said. Then he had another dream, and he told it to his brothers. 'Listen,' he said, 'I had another dream, and this time the sun and moon and eleven stars were bowing down to me.' When he told his father as well as his brothers, his father rebuked him and

*said, 'what is this dream you had? Will your mother and
I and your brothers actually come and bow down to the
ground before you?' His brothers were jealous of him,
but his father kept the matter in mind."* Genesis 37:1-11
NIV

The Bible's telling of the story of Joseph is perhaps
the best example of a dreamer with a dream that needed
tailoring. Why do I suggest tailoring dreams? It's
because when you first tell people about your dream, it
normally makes no sense to them or even to you for that
matter. It's too big; it doesn't fit. Even with Moses and
his experience at the burning bush (Exodus 3:2-15), he
was astonished at what God was calling him to do,
Moses' initial response was, "Who am I…" (Exodus
3:11). That is the same response many of us have when
we first start digesting our dream. "Who am I to try this?
How can I accomplish it? Is this really even possible?
Am I capable of such things?" The answer to all is yes.
You are indeed capable of becoming exactly what you
hope to be. But your dream must be cut to your size; it
must be tailored. That process happens through your life
experiences. What you see as failures or "bad days"
cause you to grow into your destiny. That's why in the
beginning you will encounter so much resistance—from
your friends, family, and even in your own mind.

Joseph had three things that were the ingredients for
making him into a "dream maker." He had favor
(Genesis 37:3), as his father loved him more than any of
his other sons. You too have favor, as God loves you
more than any of his other creations. He loves you more
than angels, animals, even the earth itself. But it doesn't

always feel like you have favor. Maybe you live in a single-parent home, or don't have much money. Maybe you have both parents, but they work so much that you feel like you are lacking their attention. Maybe you have lost a loved one, have an incarcerated parent, or have health issues. Whatever your problems are, know that just as in the process of planting a harvest, the seed (you) has to be planted in the soil (your origin, present life) and grow through the manure (the opposition to your dream).

Harvesting Life Experiences: Favor, Friction and an Oversized Dream

Joseph's brothers hated him because of his favor (Genesis 32:4), and hated him even the more, because of his dream (Genesis 32:8). The three necessary ingredients to becoming a dream maker are:

Understanding that your life has God's favor. This is the Romans 8:28 Principle, which states that, "All things work together for the good of them, that love God, and are called to his purpose." God's purpose, and plan is supreme, meaning it will come to pass. It is working continually in every life situation to convert everything into something that's for your good. It's like if you ever bake a cake, the final product tastes great, but each ingredient separately doesn't taste good. Flour by itself, vanilla by itself, raw eggs by themselves, are not appetizing. But the combined ingredients, mixed in a bowl and then baked in an oven, all contribute to the finished product of the cake. That's how the favor of God works—The Holy Spirit takes each ingredient in your life and combines and mixes them together to make your destiny.

Opposition is the second thing needed to become a dream maker. Although you normally hear about people trying to reduce or eliminate friction, it actually has some important uses. Since friction is a resistance force that slows down or prevents motion, it is necessary in many applications where you might want to hold unto items or do things to prevent slipping or sliding. It is the action of one source or another rubbing against each other, there is an advantage of having friction. It is sometimes called the scientific "necessary evil." Friction or opposition in dream making is necessary because it is what keeps you focused. If all you had were people cheering for you and telling you how good you were, if no one ever challenged you or looked down on you, you would never really try to become any better than what you are. Now while opposition is important, it's only useful when used correctly.

Don't let people who tease and bully hold you down or get you depressed. You have to remind yourself that the Romans 8:28 Principle is always at work in your life and that the opposition—the teasing, the testing—is meaningful if in your future it's converted to good. You get teased because you're different. Teasing and bullying is about focusing on whoever is the "oddball" in the group, the person that's different, especially when attempting to live righteously. So if everyone else is tall and you're short, they tease you. If you are tall and everyone is shorter they tease you. But the same thing they use to pick on you about is what God will use to glorify you. *"The stone the builders rejected has become the cornerstone; the Lord has done this, and it is mar- velous in our eyes. The Lord has done it this very day; let us rejoice today and be glad."* Psalm 118:22-24 NIV

The third thing you need is an oversized dream. Dreams are not one size fits all. They should not make sense at first. Joseph had a dream that he just couldn't keep to himself. Joseph had a dream, told his brothers; had another dream, and told his brothers, and parents, too. His dream was so exciting, so huge, that he just couldn't keep it to himself. Your dream is something you have to love. You have to be willing to suffer for your dreams, lose friends for your dream. Do you love your dream enough to spend more time studying so your parents will be OK with you spending so much time pursuing that God-given dream? When God gives you vision, it is life changing.

Tailored **Dreams**

three
Barriers to Success

On the road to living a life wearing your tailored dream, you must get rid of the extra fabric. Fabric is what any piece of clothing is made of. Whether it's cotton, silk, polyester, or wool, what you wear is made of something.

Similarly, your character is what you are made of, and your character is a collection of habits. Habits aren't all bad. Grooming ourselves, driving home a certain way, even brushing our teeth are habits. One of the things that you must consider in beginning to tailoring your dreams is identifying and accessing your barriers to success. What are you in the habit of doing? Studies have shown it takes 21 days to make or break a habit, 21 days to start or stop doing something, habitually. I want you to think about where you want to be in your life. Really, *imagine it*. Close your eyes and think about this day, five years from now. How old will you be? What kind of clothes are you wearing? What kind of car do you own? Where do you live? Are you in college? Did you graduate college? What do you do for a living?

I call this process "Snapshot." It's literally you taking

a mental picture of your dream. I usually suggest that you first make a "vision-board" showcasing what the answers to those questions are because that visual will serve as motivation. Next, I want you to explore what I call the 90/90 Plan. This is the method that I use to help people convert barriers into hurdles. It's really simple— 90 minutes a day for 90 days, you are to focus on developing a habit that will contribute to making your dream a reality. The 90 minutes can be broken up into three sets of 30 minutes, six sets of 15 minutes, or one 90-minute time block. But I need you to schedule these sets and stick to them. During that scheduled time, you will read, write, create, study—in other words, some activity related to developing a habit or skill that will contribute to your success. The goal is to do this for 90 days at a time. Each 90-day sequence is the "tailoring" of your dream. It's the part you play in making your dream a reality.

While we've been discussing positive habits, I want you also to consider which negative habits you need to eliminate as well. Who are the people, what are the places and things that are keeping you from your dreams? More specifically, what are the barriers? This process is called "Managing your Nouns" (people, places and things) and "Managing your Verbs" (actions).

The people you associate with, the places where you spend most of your time, and the things you do all contribute to your becoming who you are called to become and who you want to be. What most often is missed, however—when we consider this who, what, when, where, why and how—is the reality that, in most cases, *our biggest barrier is ourselves.* A barrier is anything that is standing between you and the life you want to live. Even if you think the barrier is another person, a part of that barrier is still attributed to how *you are dealing with that person.* The goal is to convert barriers into hurdles—that is, succeeding in managing to leap or scale the barriers.

Called to Endure

"SO YOU, my son, be strong (strengthened inwardly) in the grace (spiritual blessing) that is [to be found only] in Christ Jesus. And the [instructions] which you have heard from me along with many witnesses, transmit and entrust [as a deposit] to reliable and faithful men who will be competent and qualified to teach others also. Take [with me] your share of the hardships and suffering [which you are called to endure] as a good (first-class) soldier of Christ Jesus."
2 Timothy 2:1-3

Called. Purpose. Destiny. These are all buzz words that we use to describe the intent of our creation. As humans it's natural to get to a point where you want to know why you were created, was it on purpose? Did God really intentionally cause the courtship and consummation of your parents' love so that the genetic code necessary to create you, and all of your uniqueness, could exist? If that's true why couldn't that same God in his perfect nature create a life without pain, without poverty, illness, and disappointment? Because those things are ingredients in the recipe or plan for your life.

Paul said in 2 Corinthians 12:8, that he asked God three times to remove the thorn from his flesh, God's reply was that, "My grace is sufficient for you" and then added "my strength is made perfect in weakness."

This is the key to enduring the "road" to success or carrying the "weight" of your "call."

Understanding that it's not perfection that qualifies you for the call, it's your imperfections. It's you understanding that you are not flawless, but that you serve a flawless God. The power is knowing that your purpose is NOT to be perfect, but your purpose is to serve a perfect God. In serving this perfect God he has promised enough grace to cover you, and keep you, he has predestined and equipped you to live up to your call.

Your purpose is NOT to be strong. God's strength is made perfect in your weakness, so that means that when you realize an area of weakness in your life, you are really realizing an area of God's strength. How do I know what I am called to do? How do I know what my purpose is? Your calling, your purpose, your mission if you choose to accept it, lies in what causes you the most pain or irritation. We all see the world and notice different things. The thing you notice that doesn't seem to bother anyone else (but you can't get it off your mind) is at least part of your assignment. You noticed it, because God made you in such a way that your purpose acts like a family dog when it sees its master. The dog barks and jumps and shows excitement. Your purpose jumps in your spirit and soul when it recognizes its assignment—the thing it was created to address. Imagine how Michael Jordan or Kobe Bryant felt when they first held a basketball, or how Vincent van Gogh felt when he held a paint brush, or how a florist feels with flowers, or how anyone who is great at something, anyone who is working in their calling feels when they encounter their assignment.

Purpose is to assignment as clothes or fashion is to the proper season or occasion. Just as a tuxedo is meant for formal and khakis are meant for casual wear, or wool is for winter while linen is for summer months, you were designed or tailored to conquer a specific set of issues (during a specific season). There is something in the world that will only be made better because of you. Will everyone know that you are the one who changed it? Will the history books record your name? Maybe, maybe not, but the joy you will have living a tailored life is un-matched. A tailored life or living tailored dreams as we define it means:

1. A vision of a predestined outcome designed by God for a specific person and a specified time.

2. Aligning one's lifestyle to fit the God-ordained pur-pose for his/her life, living spiritually tailored.

That means organizing your life in such a way that you are in every moment living to please God and fulfill HIS will for your life. This will not be easy. The enemy, the devil, will try to stop you, but you are able to endure, because you were called to this and cut or designed for this.

Tailored Dreams

four
What Does He Call You? (The Fabric)

"Before I formed you in the womb I knew you, before you were born I set you apart; I appointed you as a prophet to the nations." "Alas, Sovereign Lord," I said, "I do not know how to speak; I am too young." But the Lord said to me, "Do not say, 'I am too young.' You must go to everyone I send you to and say whatever I command you. Do not be afraid of them, for I am with you and will rescue you," declares the Lord. Then the Lord reached out his hand and touched my mouth and said to me, "I have put my words in your mouth. See, today I appoint you over nations and kingdoms to uproot and tear down, to destroy and overthrow, to build and to plant."
Jeremiah 1:5-10 NIV

God has a plan for your life. Be intentional in uncovering it. You weren't born in it; you were sown in it. You were meant to grow through the concrete and become the rose. Where you started is not where you'll finish. For instance, my own personal story is proof of what your life can become once God gets a hold of it.

I always feel anxiety when writing about my "salvation experience" as it's not a pretty story. It's not all choirs and angels. It's more of a retelling of a journey taken by many men like me, that have come together to make the man I am today. I don't know where to start, so I guess the beginning will do…

I always say that I was too good to be considered a bad kid, but then also too bad to really be accurately described as a good kid. It took my mom three days to name me, I was born premature, and breech. The doctors told my mom I would not make it. Then once I survived birth, the new diagnosis was that I would be severely disabled and probably not be able to speak or I would have all kinds of health issues. But for God, this might have been true. It was from hearing the retelling of my birth narrative that my mom instilled in me an unwavering faith in God—at least unwavering through most of my life.

God has you here for a reason: He called me Friend…

My story is the textbook illustration of Proverbs 22:6, where it instructs parents to: *"Train up a child in the way he should go: and when he is old he will not depart from it."* My mom's a preacher, my dad's a preacher, my step mom's a preacher, so I was determined to show the world that I wasn't going to be a preacher. I grew up loving God; I learned the scriptures as quickly and could recite them as clearly as young children learn nursery rhymes. But somehow around the age of 18, despite the proper parenting and training I received from my mom, I made a conscious decision to doubt God, and decided that I might as well choose to be "unsaved"—after all, there were so many "fake" people in church.

I was the real life version of the prodigal son, wasting my life with riotous living. I clubbed, I drank alcohol, was sexually promiscuous and even experimented with marijuana. Then one night around 12:52 a.m. on June 2, 2002, I finally met God for myself. After leaving a party with friends, I sat in the passenger seat of my boy's Isuzu Rodeo, unaware that my life was about to take a major turn. My friend, who unlike me was completely sober, still managed to run a red light. In that instant a truck struck the car we were in, and all of the damage was centered right where I was seated. Our car flipped upside down and wrapped around a telephone pole. No one, not even the EMT on duty, understood how we made it out of that accident. That was the first time I had directly experienced God's protection for myself. I wish I could say that after that incident I immediately rededicated my life to Christ and lived happily ever after, but then it wouldn't be a very good story if it had such a predictable and happy ending. That day was the beginning of a change in my life—but just the beginning. It was my personal Damascus road experience, God's attempt to get my attention. It worked. It was the first time I had been confronted with my mortality. But God was just beginning his work on me…

I base my life, and the call for how to lead my life, on a statement made to me by the EMT that night once I regained consciousness. He said, "I'm an atheist, so I don't believe in God. But God has you here for a reason." I couldn't reconcile why I received such a faithful God. I didn't deserve it, I thought at the time.

But then God gives us grace, and that situation among other times in my life, helped me understand that grace really is favor we don't deserve. In the months following that incident I came across this scripture, which has since helped provide a springboard for the thesis statement of my salvation and calling: *"But by the grace of God I am what I am: and his grace which was bestowed upon me was not in vain; but I labored more abundantly than they all: Yet not I, but the grace of God which was with me."* 1 Corinthians 15:10 NIV

In the years following, I tried time and time again, to commit fully to God. But I always seemed to get frustrated and give up hope, and kept returning to my wicked ways. When I made that decision to walk away from God, no one told me it would be so hard to walk back. That reversal was a sort of "walk of shame" because I was suddenly so afraid of what people would think about me, the same guy from the club a week ago, now proclaiming the gospel of Jesus Christ. I thought they'd call me a hypocrite, as they'd remember aspects of my party reputation, and even call me crazy. But then the Holy Spirit gave me another thought in the form of a question: "What does He call you?" I began to read my bible and search for the answer.

My first stop was at John 15:15-16, and I found out that He called me friend. I realized that God, the creator of heaven and earth, considered me a friend. And to me, friend means, a person who sees you're good, witnessed your bad, and loves you anyway. I took solace in the thought that God was my friend, and that fueled a deeper understanding of the terms "grace and mercy." That is, understanding that grace is not deserving or being qualified to receive this "good thing" and receiving it anyway, while mercy was avoiding the sentence for a crime of which you are clearly guilty.

Next, I read about Jacob in Genesis 32:24-30 and saw that after Jacob wrestled all night and refused to let go, he earned a new name: God named him Israel. There are numerous stories in the Bible that illustrate a similar story: Abram to Abraham, Saul to Paul, etc., and the consistent thing was that after their personal encounter with God they were all given a new name. I heard the question again in my head, as I was sitting at a table in a café in the south of France having a conversation with God over a latte: "What does He call you?" It finally hit me that all this time God was attempting to remind me that it doesn't matter what "they" call me, or even what "I" call me. The empowering moment was when I realized that knowing how God sees me is the fuel or substance of faith. Knowing that I am the first and never the last, the head and not the tail, that God would, of course, deliver me out of peril or turmoil.

Knowing my identity in Christ pointed out that Satan was nothing more than a fraud completing "identity theft," and who had for years made me lose sight of who I was to God. It was as if I suffered from spiritual amnesia. I felt so defeated before that moment. Before I realized that the key to success in life is to answer to, and to live according to what God calls you. To commit my energy to being who God says I am. I'm still not perfect, never will be perfect at anything besides being imperfect. But yet, I still heard Him call my name. He called me redeemed; He called me restored; He called me regenerated. And He called me friend.

five
Read, React, Attack!

On January 18, 2014, I spoke to a group of teenagers at Howard University who were attending a leadership conference about the importance of being resilient. I opened by quoting "Iron" Mike Tyson, who once said, "Everybody has a plan until they get hit." That statement, in short, means that life can seem pretty easy until your dreams are met with opposition and your vision and ambition are attacked by pain.

I spoke about the importance of turning setbacks into comebacks. I explained that life would often seem unfair but that they would be ok if they learned a basic technique that coaches say to football linebackers. They are taught to "Read, react, then attack."

I walked away feeling good about myself, feeling like I had helped to encourage some students who may have needed to know the benefit of perseverance. That is until less than a week later I found myself lying in the hospital being diagnosed with an Arrhythmia, which is a rhythmic problem of the heart that can lead to stroke or heart attack. Two months later I was scheduled to have a defibrillator installed. At 33, I was facing a major setback. I had had great plans for 2014. I was supposed to release this book in April 2014, but now it was no way that was going to happen. I was the CEO of a non-profit (www.wemakedreamswork.org), and had a girlfriend to whom I wanted to propose. I had plans; surely God was playing some sort of cruel joke. You see, my plan was for 2014 to be a year of greatness, and I couldn't help but to think to myself that it was all over. Then I remembered the words I spoke to those young people. I recalled thinking that this was what Mike Tyson was talking about: I had a plan, and then got hit. Now it was time: "Read, react, and attack."

"Read" means to fully analyze the situation and look for the good. When all you see is the negative it becomes very easy to be blinded and start believing that there is no way out. That's why you have to read, read, and read again, until you find the good news. Once I read the situation properly, I discovered that though the news might at times be scary, it was not an impossible situation. I found my faith and remembered that God has the final say.

Finally, sisters and brothers, whatever is true, whatever is noble, whatever is right, whatever is pure, whatever is lovely, whatever is admirable: *If anything is excellent or praiseworthy—think about such things.* Philippians 4:8 NIV

The next phase is to "react." This means to begin to meditate on the good news. In football, a quarterback calls an "audible" when he sees that the defense has adjusted to earlier plays and is prepared to disrupt another play of the offense. The quarterback adjusts and goes to his Plan B. He calls an alternative play; he audibilizes.

Similarly, on the spot and in real time, you sometimes have to react to things in your life, and respond by beginning to edit your original plan and shaping a new one. It's all a part of the process. You have to remember that no matter how beautiful the flower is when it is in bloom, it began (germinated), in dirt, and had to grow through manure, and eventually became a beautiful flower because it was nourished and never stopped growing. *"Whatever you have learned or received or heard from me, or seen in me—put it into practice. And the God of peace will be with you."* Philippians 4:9 NIV

The third phase is to "attack." This means to merge faith with your works. By becoming an ambitious dreamer, by activating your faith, you empower your mind to create a new ending. You remix your life. Everything I thought that was lost, I overcame. I proposed to my girlfriend on June 8th, my non-profit won several major contracts and grants, including a 21st Century learning grant, and even, I wrote my first book, which you are reading now. *"I can do all this through Him who gives me strength."* Philippians 4:13 NIV

This is perhaps the most important part of tailoring your dreams; it's the part that takes the most heart. It's continually forcing yourself to advance toward your goal, while assessing potential setbacks, in real time, which requires that you quickly adjust instead of quitting. Really, at the base, we are talking about decision-making. No one ever becomes a success by accident; no one fails by accident, either. Your position in life, meaning where you ultimately "end up," is a direct result of decisions you make. Going to a party versus studying for an exam, staying up late the night before a big day, leaving your house five minutes late versus a half-hour early—all these seemingly meaningless decisions are guiding your life down a path. Your decision-making is the steering wheel on your path to dream making.

Be intentional about everything you do. Always read, react and then attack!

six
It's Not What It Looks Like

"Then Caleb silenced the people before Moses and said, "We should go up and take possession of the land, for we can certainly do it." But the men who had gone up with him said, "We can't attack those people; they are stronger than we are." And they spread among the Israelites a bad report about the land they had explored. They said, "The land we explored devours those living in it. All the people we saw there are of great size. We saw the Nephilim there (the descendants of Anak come from the Nephilim). We seemed like grasshoppers in our own eyes, and we looked the same to them." Numbers 13:30-33 NIV

This is the report of those that Moses sent to explore the Promised Land. Note they were literally at the "border of the promise." Some of us are right at the border of the promise of our lives. The thing about being at the border is that it doesn't always feel like or look like you are close to the promise.

At Kadesh-Barnea, on the border of Canaan, the people of Israel foolishly forfeited their opportunity to enter the Promised Land and claim their inheritance. This tragic failure has made the name "Kadesh" a synonym for defeat and lost opportunity. Israel's downfall was a condition of their *Visual Perception*. Visual perception is the ability to interpret the surrounding environment by processing information that is contained in visible light. In other words, visual perception is how eyesight works. The men were simply telling it the way they saw it. "We *seemed* like grasshoppers in *our own eyes*, and we *looked the same* to them."

The problem is that they had not yet learned that in order to possess what God has for you, you have to walk by faith and not by sight. Walking by faith creates a *Visual Illusion*. A visual illusion is characterized by visually perceived images that differ from objective reality. The information gathered by the eye is processed in the brain to give a perception, a sense that does not tally with a physical measurement of the stimulus source. That's why Caleb's report could be different than everyone else's, he was able to tap into his *faith sight*—walking by faith means literally reminding yourself that it's not what it looks like.

Visual perception says you look like grasshoppers, while visual illusion says, "We should go up and take possession of the land, for we can certainly do it." The problem is that we don't know what to do when what we see doesn't match what God said. We have to remember that the same God that brought you out can bring you in, such as out of Egypt into the Promised Land!

They had been in the wilderness so long that they were conditioned to not being able to go past provision to the promise. They had forgotten who the God was that made the promise, and they didn't realize they were right on the border of the place God promised Abraham he would give them. God did not allow your deliverance to merely give you "existence" or a wilderness. No, there remains a promise, a hope. Jesus said, "I am come that they might have life and have it more abundantly."

Rise and Give Praise: From Provision to Promise

The last thing we have to do in order to possess the promise is to never forget to jump. *"We seemed like grasshoppers in our own eyes, and we looked the same to them."*

When I saw this, I remembered the tragic metaphor about what happens when you put a grasshopper in a jar. Put a grasshopper in a jar, close the lid, and watch what happens. A grasshopper that repeatedly tries to jump and hits its head on the lid of a jar will eventually quit trying to jump. Because every time the grasshopper tries to do what it was born to do, it is met with opposition that limits how high and how far it can go. At some point, the grasshopper who was created and designed to jump and hop as high as it can and as often as it wants, will no longer even try because the will to do what it was created to do is gone.

In other words, don't let the ups and downs of life, the obstacles, stop you from doing what you were created to do. You, we, were created to praise, we were designed by God to give a praise that even angels can't give because we are redeemed.

I know you've been in your jar of discontent and disappointment for so long. But if you can just remember the grasshopper, and how you were created to jump, then jump to your feet and praise God in the midst of your circumstances. Jump as high as you can and praise your way out of provision straight to the promise.

seven
Wrong Place; Right Time

*"But there are some Jews whom you have set over the
affairs of the province of Babylon—Shadrach, Meshach
and Abednego—who pay no attention to you, Your
Majesty. They neither serve your gods nor worship the
image of gold you have set up." Furious with rage,
Nebuchadnezzar summoned Shadrach, Meshach and
Abednego. So these men were brought before the king,
and Nebuchadnezzar said to them, "Is it true, Shadrach,
Meshach and Abednego, that you do not serve my gods
or worship the image of gold I have set up? Now when
you hear the sound of the horn, flute, zither, lyre, harp,
pipe and all kinds of music, if you are ready to fall down
and worship the image I made, very good. But if you do
not worship it, you will be thrown immediately into a
blazing furnace. Then what god will be able to rescue
you from my hand?" Shadrach, Meshach and Abednego
replied to him, "King Nebuchadnezzar, we do not need to
defend ourselves before you in this matter. If we are
thrown into the blazing furnace, the God we serve is able
to deliver us from it, and he will deliver us from Your
Majesty's hand. But even if he does not, we want you to
know, Your Majesty, that we will not serve your gods or*

worship the image of gold you have set up." Daniel 3:12-18 NIV

According to studies by Pew Charitable Trust, and several articles published by CNN and the Huffington Post, my generation, yes, my generation, despite having one foot in Generation X, tend to identify most strongly with the attitudes and the ethos of the millennial generation. While I wrote my first essay with pen and paper, I do the majority of my sermon prep using apps like Logos and YouVersion. Even Microsoft Office I normally use from the comfort of my cell phone. We, the millennial generation—which means you were born between 1981 and the early 2000's—seems to represent an ongoing theme that young adults often feel like they have to choose between their intellectual integrity and their faith, between science and Christianity, between compassion and holiness.

Many of us are told through the media that any intelligent, progressive-thinking person that is seeking guidance for living their lives as one with the church are in the absolute WRONG PLACE.

This is not a new phenomenon. If you start reading in the first chapter of the book of Daniel, we find that King Nebuchadnezzar of Babylon had just defeated Judah, and along with some of the Articles from the temple of God, the king commanded his leaders to identify and bring children of noble birth that were intelligent and handsome and had no physical defect so they could serve him.

Among these young men were Daniel, Shadrach, Meshack, and Abednego. (Like others of Judah they were given Babylonian names by the king. Their given names were, respectively, Belteshazzar (Daniel), Hananiah (Shadrach), Misha-el (Meshack), and Azariah (Abednego.) In the Bible's third chapter of Daniel, we find Shadrach, Meshack, and Abednego in "the wrong place" we referenced above. They were being threatened with death for choosing not to follow the king's decrees and doing the opposite of what all in Babylonian society were commanded. Everyone else worshipped the image of the idol god that the king created.

But these young men recognized something a lot of people miss—that is, the power of choice. You can't choose what happens to you, but how you respond or recover is completely your choice. They took a stand: they decided to be one with God when everyone else was bowing to public opinion. It's not easy to maintain your faith or beliefs when society tells you what you believe is outdated and wrong. Society would like you to think that you're "in the wrong place" when you choose to stand for God. But here's the lesson: If you have faith in Him, and stay true, *God will show up in the fire.* These young men ultimately did not miss the fire. They had to go in the furnace, but they did not have to go in the furnace alone.

We all will have a furnace experience, a time when we feel like we made the right decision though still ended up in the wrong place. But don't get discouraged—even though you are in the fire, you are not alone. *When you exercise the power of choice and*

*choose to represent God, no matter what, that kind of
faith moves God to action and will ensure that He shows
up in the fire.*

Stay Wrong for God: He'll Carry You Through the Fire

This story in the Book of Daniel is instructive. The
king had issued a decree for the province of Babylon to
worship the golden image. Similarly, many in society
today will paint a picture of what they want you to value,
and if you don't bow to it, these societal forces will try
and convince you that you are wrong. But don't fall for
it: Instead, stay wrong for God, and He will make you
right.

It may get uncomfortable, but He will use your haters
to set you up for promotion, just as he did the three
young men in the book of Daniel. Shadrach, Meshack,
and Abednego had confidence in what made them
different from everyone else. They were being perse-
cuted because they believed in a God different than the
King's gods, and refused to worship the image of gold
the King had set up to be cherished. The three had full
faith that the God they believed in was able to save them
from any situation. As long as they continued to believe
in God's ability to save them, they knew that their
inability to save themselves would be handled by God.

I believe this as well. In every situation, I have
slowly learned that being on the wrong side with
everyone else is worth it, if it keeps you on the right side
with God. The thing to remember while tailoring your
dreams is that God is the tailor. Let him have full control,

and he will always lead you in the way that produces the best outcome for your life.

I know what you may be thinking; that's a lot to expect from a teenager, from a young adult. You might be saying to yourself, "I just want to be normal." At least that was what I wanted; to be like everyone else. But being like everyone else is not the destiny of a tailored dreamer. You are special; you have a specific purpose that God wants to fulfill in your life. He wants to not only show up in the furnace for you, but He wants to vindicate you. For every moment you felt awkward, and didn't quite fit in, for every time you listened to the Holy Spirit and didn't go where everyone else was going, He would make it worthwhile. After Shadrach, Meshack, and Abednego went through the furnace, they were promoted. Elevation is always preceded by a period of separation. But believe me, it's worth it in the end.

Who We Are "Post to Be"...

This brings me to my grandmother, Ruth M. Bradley. She was a source of great inspiration for me, and a lot of things to many people. She was a wife, then a widow; a daughter, a mother, a grandmother; a church mother, a church musician, and a dedicated neighborhood watch before it had a name.

No matter what question I, or anyone, could think to ask for advice, her answer never changed. She'd say, "Honey, let The Lord do it," and I would get so upset because I would want what I thought was "real" advice. I wanted her to give me step-by-step directions on how to do what I was asking. Instead, she gave me what I thought at the time were empty words—"Let The Lord do it." Well, I would soon find out how powerful those words were.

My Grandmother passed away in 1997, on October 24. I will never forget that date because I was the one who found her. Immediately, I missed her. I didn't understand why she had to go so soon. Her funeral was held a little over a week later on October 31, at the church she attended all of my life. It was a small church, but that day, even if it were a mega church, it would've been inadequate. Literally hundreds of people showed up to pay their respects to a woman who most said they had only met once or twice—most were outside of the group of people that I had met before. Some remembered her as the kind woman on the bus or train who sparked up a conversation with a stranger. Then if the person said they were in the least bit in need, they recalled her as saying, "Well, let The Lord do it." But she never left it with just that. She would then call someone who could help the person, right then, immediately. Person after person remembered her doing that *every day of her life.* She wasn't famous, but she knew her purpose, which was to "Let The Lord do it." No matter what "it" was, she was determined to let God use her to "do it." And if there is one major lesson I learned from my grandmother it was to say where and what you are "post to be." In other words, "supposed to be." She had no reservations about being completely who God called her to be. In an age when so much of our lives are played out via social media, I wonder how many of us are actually the same person that we are perceived to be from what we "post" or who we are "post to be?"

"You will be betrayed, even by parents, brothers and sisters, relatives and friends and they will put some of you to death. Everyone will hate you because of me. But not a hair of your head will perish. Stand firm, and you will win life." Luke 21:16-19 NIV

Omarion has a song out called "post to be," and one of the lyrics says, "If your girl comes close to me/she won't come home where she's post to be." Well, God asked me to drop the remix on you: If you don't remember anything else, He wants you to remember that: *"If you just 'stay wrong' with me, I will always show up, where I'm 'post to be.' If you keep your faith in me, you will always be where you 'post to be.'"* That's how the Hebrew boys could have faith: They knew what their God was capable of, and that even if they ended up in the fire, they would be OK because that would be where they were post to be. That's why Stephen, an apostle of an early Christian church (Acts: 7 NIV), could stay in the spirit even while being stoned—he was preaching while they were stoning because he knew that even though the media said he was in the wrong place, he knew Jesus would stand for him, that Jesus would save him at the right time, because he stayed right where he was "post to be."

Tailored Dreams

eight
Traffic Jam (You were cut for this)

"Here comes that dreamer!" they said to each other. "Come now, let's kill him and throw him into one of these cisterns and say that a ferocious animal devoured him. Then we'll see what comes of his dreams." Genesis 37:19-20 NIV

A sad fact is that most people settle for simply making a living instead of living a life. The difference is living a life solely rooted in making money, solely dependent upon a career. You go to school and get good grades so you can go to a better school, including graduate school, learn more and get a really good job and make a lot of money and suddenly become happy. Only the problem is that even some of the richest and most educated people find themselves unhappy. That's because happiness does not depend entirely on money or book learning alone.

While money is important, a more important part of being happy is related to living a full life. The biggest mistake is thinking the American Dream is just the house and picket fence. It's also the intangible things that make that house the home you want to come home to. Yes, education is important, and working and making money is important, but so is asking yourself what *truly* is important: Why am I here?

A good way to figure out purpose is to ask what is it you would do if money were no issue. If you were rich and didn't need money, what would you wake up every day and do for free? Because for some of us our purpose is connected to our careers and we may be able to make a living from it, but in most cases it starts out being something you do because you are in love with doing it, and would do it whether you earn a great amount of money or not. It "makes a living" because it makes life worth living.

I am in love with motivating people. I truly believe part of my purpose is to help guide others toward achieving their "natural full self." Your natural full self is the most authentic and complete "you" you can be.

James Truslow Adams, the founding father I quoted in chapter one on the American Ethos, also said that he believed we should all have two educations: One that teaches us how to make a living, and the other to teach us how to live. I too am a firm believer in this. The house with the picket fence, two car garages, and all the money in the world are worthless without them being a part of a life—a life connected to friends, family, community; a life filled with the pursuit of happiness.

Regarding this pursuit of happiness, there will be

many times when your road seems to be leading you in the complete opposite direction of where God promised to take you. Revisiting the story of Joseph, we find his brothers plotting to kill him. Even before Joseph arrives, the Romans 8:28 Principle intervenes: *"When Reuben heard this, he tried to rescue him from their hands. "Let's not take his life," he said. "Don't shed any blood. Throw him into this cistern here in the wilderness, but don't lay a hand on him." Reuben said this to rescue him from them and take him back to his father."* Genesis 37:21-22 NIV

Centered on Doing Your Father's Business

God uses Joseph's brother Reuben to influence the other brothers to spare his life. Similarly, we all go through tough periods when it seems like our dreams are dying, and are simply "traffic jams." Just like when you are in a car on your way somewhere important and the trip starts out great, and it looks like you'll arrive early with time to spare, then suddenly the cars ahead begin to slow, and for a moment you really think you won't make it on time. You are caught in traffic. You are on a road cluttered with other travelers. But you have to stay calm—the traffic jam lasts just a moment, not forever. My mother raised me with a principle that helped me embrace when life presents a delay on my path. She always said, "Son, take every delay as of the Lord." I would always think, "What!?! But I'm going to be late." Sometimes being just five minutes late can make you miss a car crash, or help you meet someone that can change your life. Being late can sometimes be a blessing. It's in the traffic jams of life that God often is able to do his best work tailoring lives. In those moments when things slow up or stop for a bit, we become a captive audience and God can really begin to cut away things in our lives that need to change.

There are three things that can happen in traffic. Those three things happen because you are able to finally have uncomfortable conversations with yourself or rather you are finally listening to the beckoning and pleading of the Holy Spirit. Consider:

1. How to overcome other people's opinions of your dream. Think about it, before Joseph even arrived they saw him coming and got angry, "The Dreamer cometh," they said with scorn. They didn't believe his dream. It upset them. The reality is that people are not really mad at you for dreaming, they aren't mad at your dream. They are mad at your audacity to actually believe your dream can become a reality. How dare you think that God has enough power to give you vision and provision!

2. You learn to replace your fear with faith. Dreaming is scary business. It's literally peeping into the possibility and seeing it as probability. It's believing your life can one day be different, deeper, and vastly more abundant than it is now. But what if you're wrong? What if it doesn't work out? Won't people laugh at you? Won't you look stupid? That's fear. "What ifs" can be fear or reason. The way to tell the difference is if the "what if's" are challenging you to quit or challenging you to audit or evaluate your approach. There is nothing wrong with logic and reasoning helping you to make better decisions; however, quitting is the assassination of your dreams. Don't allow your position to dictate your perception—instead use your perception to define your position. In other words, don't allow what you see to make you too fearful to try. Instead use the fear in what you see as fuel for your ambition to reach your goals.

3. Practice Crowd Control. Learning to filter both the compliments and condemnation from those in your life is critical, that's why I speak of practicing "Crowd Control." The crowd has nothing to do with you achieving your crown. Giving too much attention to the praise people give you is just as hazardous as giving into fear. Be careful not to believe your own hype. God exalts the humble, not the proud. Keep your mind centered on doing your father's business. Your dream coming true isn't for you to get credit. God and you do the work and the glory goes to God only. The dream is another tool to give God the glory, as God will make sure you get glory from him, not the crowd.

Tailored **Dreams**

nine
The Royal Class

"But you are a chosen generation, a royal priesthood, a holy nation, His own special people, that you may proclaim the praises of Him who called you out of darkness into His marvelous light; who once were not a people but are now the people of God, who had not obtained mercy but now have obtained mercy." 1 Peter 2:9, 10 NIV

Have you ever really considered what it means to be royal? You are chosen. There is no part of you or your life that was accidental, or coincidental. You were selected. God was so intentional in His designing of you, that He made sure that every detail necessary for creating you was in place. Take the story of King David. It begins in 1 Samuel the 16th chapter, when David was anointed. He like some of us wasn't the ideal candidate, but he would become a man and king after God's own heart. *"But the Lord said to Samuel, 'Do not consider his appearance or his height, for I have rejected him. The Lord does not look at the things people look at. People look at the outward appearance, but the Lord looks at the heart.'"* 1 Samuel 16:10-12 NIV

On your pathway to your throne consider this: You will at times experience failure, but failure is not a wall; it is a gateway to the next level. Failure is life's best teacher. So don't stay married to your present, don't allow yourself to be a prisoner of your past—you have the opportunity to become the architect of your future.

You are not just descended from Kings and Queens— you are royalty. Your life is your kingdom, and your kingdom is inhabited by your dreams. The enemy to your kingdom is any distraction that threatens to deter you from accomplishing your dreams. One of the biggest threats to our personal success is stage fright. It's our fear of what the crowd will think. We become ruled by our fear instead of being rulers over our fear.

If you understand that you are royalty then you accept that you are "crowd shifters." What is a crowd shifter? It's a person that shows up and changes the atmosphere. You can feel their presence in a room. That's who and what you were created to be. You were designed to shift crowds not flow with them. Your sheer presence was designed to make people take notice: "Stop, Look, and Listen" is your imprint. When you show up, the room immediately pauses. That's the King and Queen in you.

It's the same quality that often makes it hard for you to fit in. Being of royalty isn't easy. It's quite uncomfortable at times, but it's worth it. When you are a specialty item, you aren't often easily found amongst other items on the "rack." Indeed, you are found in a tailor's shop, not a department store. You define your situations; you do not allow your situations to define you.

You were designed to rule. Being royal is more than a notion; it's a full-time commitment to gradually becoming who God created you to be. David was anointed to be King and then went back to being a Shepard, then a solider. It was a long road between being anointed as king and being ready to actually be the king. Enjoy the process, but commit to progress.

Tailored Dreams

ten
Be the Brand

"Therefore, if anyone is in Christ, the new creation has come: The old has gone, the new is here! All this is from God, who reconciled us to himself through Christ and gave us the ministry of reconciliation: that God was reconciling the world to himself in Christ, not counting people's sins against them. And he has committed to us the message of reconciliation. We are therefore Christ's ambassadors, as though God were making his appeal through us. We implore you on Christ's behalf: Be reconciled to God. God made him who had no sin to be sin for us, so that in him we might become the righteousness of God." 2 Corinthians 5:17-21 NIV

What does it mean to be a brand? Or even a brand ambassador? A brand is defined as a name, term, design, symbol, or any other feature that identifies one seller's goods or service from those of other sellers. For instance what is the visual that comes to mind when you think of Coke or Pepsi, Nike or Reebok? The visual representation you thought of is the brand, and the person you associate with those brands is the brand ambassador. Have you ever considered that you are a representation of a brand as a Christian? Well, you are—

this is the 5:20 Principle: *"We are therefore Christ's ambassadors, as though God were making his appeal through us."* What is the appeal? *"We implore you on Christ's behalf: Be reconciled to God."*

This is what we are supposed to represent, at all times. Jesus is alive in us, and our actions day-to-day may be the only "Jesus" this generation ever sees. So it is our duty to "rep the brand"; it is our responsibility to be aware that people are looking at us as the representatives for a God they don't know, or don't believe in. This doesn't mean that we are supposed to be perfect. It means that more and more we should be like Christ. How do we become like Christ? *"A new command I give you: Love one another. As I have loved you, so you must love one another. By this everyone will know that you are my disciples, if you love one another."* John 13:34-35 NIV

We represent the brand, the brand being Jesus, with our love for one another. Love, not judgment, not condemnation, but by our love. By repping the brand, we get to help other people to learn how to tailor their dreams, how to make their lives whole. What comes to people's minds after they meet you? What do they associate you with?

Here's a test: Ask a few people of their first impression of you, then ask them what gives them that impression. This serves as a guide to know what kind of message your life is communicating to others every day, as you attempt to represent God, your family and your dreams. It would be horrible to do all this hard work and then not get to see your dream come into fruition simply because of a reputation, especially if that reputation is not representative of who you really are. Your life, His Brand. Think about that: It's your life, you are free to live it as you want. You don't have to care what people think about you. But it's His brand, His blood that was shed to give you grace and mercy that paves the way to access to a better life. You are Christ ambassadors—it's as if He was making His appeal directly through you. What appeal can God make through your life? What do people see about God through you? How are you repping the brand?

Living our daily lives, allowing God to work in and through our lives, is us repping the brand. We will encounter opposition. Consider the story of Lazarus told in the book of John, the 11th chapter. Here we find one of Jesus' friends, the Bible refers to him as the one Jesus loves. He was sick, and then died. Jesus went and resurrected him. He brought his friend who was sick and died, back to life. Lazarus was a great brand ambassador. But how? What did he really do? He just got sick; he just died. OK, fine, he came back to life. But no, Jesus brought him to life. So what did he, Lazarus, do, and how do we know Lazarus had any real impact on anyone's life? *"Meanwhile a large crowd of Jews found out that Jesus was there and came, not only because of him but also to see Lazarus, whom he had raised from the dead. So the chief priests made plans to kill Lazarus as well, for on account of him many of the Jews were going over to Jesus and believing in him."* John 12:9-11 NIV.

Tailored Dreams

eleven
God's Mathematics

"Joseph said to his brothers, "I am Joseph! Is my father still living?" But his brothers were not able to answer him, because they were terrified at his presence. Then Joseph said to his brothers, "Come close to me." When they had done so, he said, "I am your brother Joseph, the one you sold into Egypt! And now, do not be distressed and do not be angry with yourselves for selling me here, because it was to save lives that God sent me ahead of you." Genesis 45:3-5 NIV

God has a way of making things turn around, and all make sense in the end. I call it "God's Mathematics." God will often subtract before he adds, he will divide before he multiplies, but in the end it all adds up.

Joseph was 17 when he was sold into Egypt.

He was 30 when he was made overseer.

He was 39 when his brothers first came to Egypt (second year of the famine, or nine years after being made overseer).

He was probably 41 or so when the brothers came a second time and Jacob comes to Egypt.

He was 110 when he died.

Stay Committed: Without Bad Days, There Are No Best Days

By following this timeline, we see only Joseph's victories. That's the same way social media works. We only see what people post about their lives, and therefore, if we are not careful we will become envious of such people without the benefit of their whole story. That's because, we very rarely post our struggles. Joseph had a dream at 17 that didn't fully come true until he was 41. That's a lot of time. The timeline doesn't show his brothers tossing him into the pit, or his boss's wife lying on him and landing him in jail. But those things happened and they are also a huge part of the Romans 8:28 Principle of using those ingredients to work toward his dream coming true. It had to happen just like that, because without him experiencing any one of those "bad days," he would not have had any of his best days.

How did Joseph keep his faith and focus through such hardship? He never forgot the playbook. A playbook in sports is a book that contains the plans or plays designed to help the team win the game. Every player on the team has a role, or an assignment. Any one player not running the play or their part of the play correctly, results in a loss of yards, the other team advancing or scoring, or simply put, a failed play. In order to fully take advantage of the math God has planned for your life, you must learn the playbook, or the promises of God that are found in the Bible. You can even simply Google "God's promises" and begin to study. God's promises are as exact as the laws of physics and serve a similar purpose as an offensive line in football. God's promises create holes in the defense, blocks defenders, and helps recover from fumbles. God's grace, which works to fuel the math, makes it possible for you to call an audible. Calling an audible is simply changing the play at the line of scrimmage. In real life it means going to your plan b or plan c to be successful in accomplishing your goals. Faith accompanied with hard work creates what in football is called the "YAC"—yards after the catch—that means you ran the play, threw the ball, caught the ball, and now what? Do you settle for the yardage received from simply catching the ball, or do you push forward for the extra yards after the catch? You go for the extra yards. Every yard is important to earning a victory in a football game, and every minute you dedicate to achieving your dream is vital to your success. This is what I call "4th quarter dreaming." Dreaming with your back against the wall, pushing past your fear of what others are saying and doing the work that it takes to achieve your dream. It's not just important to believe you can achieve it, you have to actually stand there, face the defense, and run the ball straight up the middle through the defense and across the goal line to a score.

Score, that just really means never breaking your word to yourself. Whatever you said you were going to accomplish, you stay committed to making that thing happen. And when you do that consistently, you're one step closer to living a tailored dream.

Tailored Dreams

twelve
Your Greater Good Life (Dream Maker)

"The thief comes only to steal and kill and destroy; I have come that they may have life, and have it to the full. "I am the good shepherd. The good shepherd lays down his life for the sheep. The hired hand is not the shepherd and does not own the sheep. So when he sees the wolf coming, he abandons the sheep and runs away. Then the wolf attacks the flock and scatters it. The man runs away because he is a hired hand and cares nothing for the sheep. "I am the good shepherd; I know my sheep and my sheep know me—just as the Father knows me and I know the Father—and I lay down my life for the sheep."
John 10:10-15 NIV

The real way to tailor your dreams is to make sure you have a relationship with the Dream Maker. God is the Dream Maker. He is the author and finisher of your faith. Jesus said that he has come so that you might have life and have it more abundantly. That means not only that you will be alive, but also it is God's will for you to live abundantly. Which is living out your purpose. God created you, designed your dream, and has been through the Romans 8:28 Principle, continuously tailoring your life to fit your dreams. That's right, God cares about your dreams; He cares about what you want your life to be because He gave you the desire. That is, as long as you have allowed God into your life. That's salvation— salvation is the "that they might have life" part. The second part is your relationship with God the father and his unfailing love; with Christ the son, and his grace and mercy; and with communion and guidance from the Holy Spirit. This is true abundant life. It's living in a covenant state with God. The "My cup runs over" that the psalmist wrote about (Psalm 23:5): *"You prepare a table before me in the presence of my enemies; You anoint my head with oil; My cup runs over."* This kind of relationship with God will cause him to use your enemies as tools for your construction instead of your destruction. This is the kind of relationship where he gives you all he's promised and then gives you overflow, or extras.

Learning all of the tools, listening to every step I have outlined in this book about tailoring dreams and not having a relationship with the Dream Maker, is like trying to win a Nascar race without a race car or driver. The thread and the needle used to tailor your life must be God. Like a real relationship with the living God, he has designed even this very moment so that you could be drawn to him. This is not me saying you are not already "saved"; remember that's life. I am asking if you believe you have an abundant life yet? An abundant life doesn't mean you don't have problems, it doesn't mean you won't feel pain. It is the assurance that the Romans 8:28 Principle is at work in your life. All things, at all times, are always working for your good, for your greater good, for your greater good life. No matter what happens, if you are in a relationship with God, then you are living the "Greater Good Life," and your steps are ordered and your life is tailored. Your dreams will come true, and each day more and more they are being tailored to you. The greater good life is the key principle in creating a tailored life. It's living an "others first" life; it's servant leadership in every area of your life. God elevates the humble, and humbles the proud. So it is impossible to never be as successful as you could truly become if you leave humility out of the equation. If you do, you cannot lead. Living balanced, taking care of your body through exercise and clean eating is actually another form of worship to God. It's thanking God for life and health through taking proper care of your body.

I thought my youth would last forever. The worst feeling ever is to be old before your time. I am currently on the road back to healthy living and eating, but years of doing the wrong thing has already had a negative impact on my life. Drinking too much, eating the wrong foods, smoking, not exercising… Remember that every action has an equal or opposite reaction. That means there is a price to pay for "doing what you want." I encourage you to embrace these teachings now as teenagers and as young adults. Form positive habits now, chase your dreams, stay connected to God, allow the Holy Spirit to tailor your dreams, and you will live an inheritance of the Greater Good Life.

Eight Day
Tailored Dreams Devotional

DAY...1

*D*o you see what I see?

"Now faith is confidence in what we hope for and assurance about what we do not see."
Hebrews 11:1 (NIV)

Faith is defined not by what is seen, but by your confidence that what is unseen will be. Your calling or purpose may not look like your present state. Right now you may be a determined young person who was cut from a basketball team, or maybe you are a 22-year-old college graduate who didn't get into the graduate school program you planned on attending. Perhaps you are an adult who is praying for a better financial situation—and your life isn't going as planned. In either case, you are not the sum total of what your current situation looks like. It really doesn't matter what it looks like. The real question is what are you willing to do to become who you are meant to be? Can you look in the mirror and see what God sees? Can you view your life through the lens of faith? Can you have confidence in what you hope for while ignoring what you see? Can you depend on God's vision as evidence of what is meant to happen?

Make time this week to write out your design of what you want your life to look like.

To begin this design, close your eyes and answer these questions:

Where do I want to live? (house, apartment, city, suburb, beach front, country)

Do I want to be a laborer or a thinker? (work hard through physical labor or be compensated for your ideas and leadership ability)

How do I want to spend my time away from work?

How will I measure success?

What type of people (or who specifically) will be in my inner-circle?

In order to accomplish this, think through "head, heart, and legs" for each item.

Head - What will I need to feed my mind in order to accomplish these tasks?
Heart - How will I build up resilience to be able to maintain emotional strength?
Legs - What habits will I need to form in order to accomplish these tasks?

Prayer starter
God guide my thoughts, feelings, and actions towards becoming the person you see when you look at me. Help my faith to sketch my path, and your law to stitch together my actions, that the life I lead may be pleasing to you... In Jesus' name, amen.

Tailored Dreams

DAY...2

$\mathcal{W}$hat's your size?

"Suppose one of you wants to build a tower. Won't you first sit down and estimate the cost to see if you have enough money to complete it? For if you lay the foundation and are not able to finish it, everyone who sees it will ridicule you, saying, 'This person began to build and wasn't able to finish."
Luke 14:28-30 (NIV)

One of the most important steps in becoming a tailored dreamer is to embrace your uniqueness. The surest way to embrace your uniqueness is to count your cost. To "count the cost" you must understand that your creator gave his son's life so that you may live life abundantly. He wouldn't do that for just anybody. He did that because you are more precious than gold. It is the most rare jewels that are worth the most money. You were created to be exactly who you are, the problem is many of us have no idea how to embrace our quirky, wonderful selves.

Knowing yourself in relation to effective dreaming is just as important as knowing what size you wear when you go shopping. As difficult as it would be to find the perfect outfit without first figuring out what size you wear, it is that much harder to live your best life without knowing the strength of your weaknesses. Yes, I said, "the strength of your weaknesses." The very thing that you were teased for, or bullied about, or ridiculed for, is the same thing God will use to elevate you. You may be the one that's too tall now but that's because you were designed to do something that requires you to have height. Romans the eighth chapter says that the sufferings of the present are in no way comparable to the glory that is coming. So how do we know our size? How do we properly design a life tailored for us? The beginning of that process is embracing what makes you unique, then praying that God shows you the strength of it, and finally understanding that your passion is hidden in your frustration. The things that irritate you about the world are the issues that you are designed and called and assigned to address.

To begin to count your cost, close your eyes and answer these questions.

What are the areas in my life that I feel insecure about, and how can I find strength in them?

What are the things that really irritate me about society in the following categories; at home, in school, in my community?

What can I do to create change, bring awareness, or have an impact in those areas?

In order to accomplish this, think through "head, heart, and legs" for each item.

Head - What will I need to feed my mind in order to accomplish these tasks?
Heart - How will I build up resilience to be able to maintain emotional strength?
Legs - What habits will I need to form in order to

accomplish these tasks?

Prayer starter
God thank you for taking time to create me as an individual. I thank you for equipping me for the life you tailored for me. I embrace my differences and find strength in my weakness. I know that when I am weak you are strong. Help me to find my purpose and embrace my uniqueness, in Jesus' name, amen.

DAY...3

I was designed for this!

"For you created my inmost being; you knit me together in my mother's womb. I praise you because I am fearfully and wonderfully made; your works are wonderful, I know that full well."
Psalm 139:13-14 (NIV)

You created my inmost being. What a statement, what a concept, to think that even your innermost parts, thoughts, emotions, feelings, likes and dislikes were all created by God, and all have a purpose. You were created to go through the things you go through, you were selected to be exactly who you are, God took his time in creating you, and he took care in making you. God considered everything you would encounter and equipped you with all you need to not just survive but to thrive. He knit you together, stitched every part of your life together for his glory before you ever left your mother's womb. That sickness you have that no other young person has to deal with, that relative that did that horrible thing to you, that bully, or that heartbreak you suffered is not the end of your story, it's not even a climatic point. Your trials do not mean that God is punishing you.

You will make it through this. You are loved, you are capable, and you will survive. God has faith in you. Yes I said God has faith in you. He knows that as hard as this is, as difficult as it is to understand you are more than the sum total of your hard times, you are bigger than your mistakes, and you are NOT a mistake. You are an intentional being created by an intentional God and every tear is watering an intended harvest. Do not let circumstances make you believe that God has passed you by or that he has circumvented your purpose. We may even at times get mad at God because it just doesn't make sense, why did this have to happen like this? Why did I have to endure this kind of pain? But there is a blessing in every storm. There is a lesson, something we learn—we begin to learn that it doesn't have to make sense for God to make it alright.

To begin to create your design, close your eyes and answer these questions:

What parts of my life am I having trouble finding purpose in?

What am I mad at God about?

What am I "faithing" and what am I fearing?

Think through the "head, heart, and legs" for each item.

Head - What will I need to feed my mind in order to accomplish these tasks?
Heart - How will I build up resilience to be able to maintain emotional strength?
Legs - What habits will I need to form in order to accomplish these tasks?

Prayer starter
God thank you for all that you have done for me. Thank

you for predestining me to be conformed to the image of your son. Thank you for writing my ending before my beginning. I exalt you and believe that your design is flawless because it is impossible for you to fail. I decree and declare my freedom from insecurity in Jesus' name, amen.

DAY...4

*C*onsider the fabric. What are you made of?

"My frame was not hidden from you when I was made in the secret place, when I was woven together in the depths of the earth. Your eyes saw my unformed body; all the days ordained for me were written in your book before one of them came to be." Psalm 139:15-16 (NIV)

Another area to understand while on your quest to becoming a tailored dreamer is embracing and understanding the value in your whole story. We all have a past. Some of us have had a rough start. Others have had a more smooth start in life. Whether your story started out rocky or as gentle as the sea, it just speaks to a portion of what you are made of. Some of us even end up with scars. Scars are just proof that we've been in a battle and made it out. You are more than a conqueror through him that loved us. You serve a God that loves you, and he loves you so much that he took care with creating every detail of your life. Just like a master tailor considers the fabric of the garment he's trying to make, God considered your fabric. He knows what you are made of. Your frame was not hidden to him. He knows every little detail of your life, "All the days ordained for me were written in your book before one of them came to be" (Psalms 139:15-16). God knew every single detail of your life before it ever happened, and he loves you, still.

We tear our fabric and cause ourselves pain because

we don't submit to God's will in and for our lives. The best move for us to make is often the most difficult, and that is to simply let the Lord do it. Open your hands and allow God to have free reign in your life. It's as if we don't understand that as our creator he is actually more qualified and equipped to handle taking the fabric of our past, tracing out the frame of our purpose, cutting away the excess material and then stitching it all together. That's why I love this scripture, *"When I was woven together in the depths of the earth"* (Psalm 139:15). It clearly depicts the care God took in creating us, and if he took that level of care in creating us, then how much more care will he give to caring for us, to tailoring us, to guiding us in the way that leads to us becoming the exact people we were designed and created to be?

To begin to consider your fabric, close your eyes and answer these questions.

What about my past scares me, and how can I use it as a testimony?

Am I relinquishing my will and surrendering to God's will in every area of my life?

How can I show or represent God's craftsmanship in my everyday life?

In order to accomplish this, think through "head, heart, and legs" for each item.

Head - What will I need to feed my mind in order to accomplish these tasks?
Heart - How will I build up resilience to be able to maintain emotional strength?

Legs - What habits will I need to form in order to accomplish these tasks?

Prayer starter

God thank you for another chance to reflect your glory. Help me to totally surrender my will to yours. I want to decrease that you might increase in me. Please allow your Holy Spirit to be the lens that the world looks through to see me. Help them to look at me but to see Jesus. I thank you for your faithfulness in my life, you were with me before my beginning and promised to never leave nor forsake me, so I give you full authority over the direction of my life, in Jesus' name, amen.

DAY...5

You ou were cut for this.

"Before I formed you in the womb I knew you, before you were born I set you apart; I appointed you as a prophet to the nations."
Jeremiah 1:5 (NIV)

There is a purpose in your struggle. A diamond is created through pressure, a pearl is created from a drop of sand getting into a clam and the pearl is birthed from the irritation. You were cut, or designed for this very dream you have. Try not to focus on what you don't have or the ways you think you are unqualified. God not only qualified you, he justified you. It doesn't matter what anyone else thinks. He made the decision to qualify you while you were still in the belly of your mother's womb, he ordained you, and he called you. And since that moment, every day that you have lived has been preparing you for the next day.

Some of the best culinary works call for some of the most bitter or tasteless ingredients. A single ingredient by itself would not be something we would want to taste, but when blended with the other ingredients it goes from a pinch of salt to a delicious chocolate cake. A raw egg by itself may be hard to digest, but when you add a few more ingredients and add heat to it, an omelet is created and has a wonderful taste. I learned a long time ago that there are no such things as good days or bad days, they are just days—days which the Lord has made, and I will rejoice and be glad "in it," all of them. Good things happen and "bad" things happen, but I refuse to say a whole day is "bad." I know that God cut me for this, that I am cut out for this, and that I will make it and become the person God has designed me to be.

To begin to remember you were cut for this, close your eyes and answer these questions.

What did God prequalify me for?
What are the bitter ingredients of my life that made life better later?
What do I have the power to do "good" everyday in spite of my feelings?

In order to accomplish this, think through "head, heart, and legs" for each item.

Head - What will I need to feed my mind in order to accomplish these tasks?
Heart - How will I build up resilience to be able to maintain emotional strength?
Legs - What habits will I need to form in order to accomplish these tasks?

Prayer starter
Lord of heaven and earth, I exalt your name; I choose to humble myself and turn to you for direction. God forgive me for my sins, and help me forgive those who sin against me. Help me to live in a way that is pleasing to you. Your word says that when a man's ways please the

Lord, he'll make even his enemies be at peace with him. I ask that you transform my enemies into supporters, and make my haters my motivators, in Jesus' name I pray, amen.

DAY...6

*S*tyle takes commitment

"Then you will call on me and come and pray to me, and I will listen to you. You will seek me and find me when you seek me with all your heart."
Jeremiah 29:12-13 (NIV)

Tailoring your dreams is a process of creating a new mind state, it's not about changing your dreams, it's about changing your habits and your thought process. You are what you do consistently. You are who you spend the most time with, what does that say about you? *Is it true that I am defined by what I do consistently?* In the aforementioned scripture it says, "You will seek me and find me when you seek me with all your heart." When you seek something with your whole heart that means you have committed to finding it and won't stop until you do.

You won't settle for any outcome other than a victorious one. Seeking God's will for your life is the only way you will be able to learn to become a tailored dreamer. God is the Tailor, you are the garment, submit to God and commit to the process, and watch God's plan begin to unfold in your life. Just as Jesus is real, the enemy is real to, and the enemy is committed to your failure. The devil desires to have you, but the good news is that God is just as confident and more committed to your success than the devil is your failure. He wants the glory. The glory is what activates your shift, and it's the catalyst for the change you want to see in your life. Will you give him the glory? Will you praise him in the middle of the storm, will you believe past belief? God wants all of you. The scripture says, "Then you will call on me and come and pray to me, and I will listen to you. You will seek me and find me when you seek me with all your heart." Sometimes it may feel like we are playing hide and seek with God, but you will find God and he will be your tailor when you seek him with all of your heart. Are you as committed to God as he is to you?

To begin to carve out your commitment, answer these questions.

Am I truly committed to God?

What am I willing to give up to get closer to God?

What is one thing I can do every day to intentionally seek to be in God's presence?

In order to accomplish this, think through "head, heart, and legs" for each item.

Head - What will I need to feed my mind in order to accomplish these tasks?
Heart - How will I build up resilience to be able to maintain emotional strength?
Legs - What habits will I need to form in order to accomplish these tasks?

Prayer starter
God I thank you for my early rising, please endow me with the power to become more like you daily. I surrender my will to your will. I commit to seeking you with my whole heart and complete soul. Father I come to

you with feeling of shame and emotional hurt. I know that you are faithful and just to forgive me, and I am full of confidence and faith knowing that when I look for you with my whole heart, I will find you, in Jesus' name, amen.

DAY...7

$\mathcal{B}$e the seed

"How foolish! What you sow does not come to life unless it dies. When you sow, you do not plant the body that will be, but just a seed, perhaps of wheat or of something else. But God gives it a body as he has determined, and to each kind of seed he gives its own body!"
Corinthians 15:36-38 (NIV)

The plant starts life as a seed, which germinates and grows into a plant. The mature plant produces flowers, which are fertilized and produce seeds in a fruit or seedpod. The plant eventually dies, leaving seeds which germinate to produce new plants. Annuals take one year to complete their life cycle.

This cycle describes the life cycle of seeds; a plant starts with a seed and still ends with a seed. It kind of reminds me of the scripture in the gospel of John the first chapter, *"In the beginning was the Word, and the Word was with God, and the Word was God. He was with God in the beginning. Through him all things were made; without him nothing was made that has been made."* Jesus was the seed, planted himself in the world germinated and grew into the true vine, and then died, and rose again, but then left us with the capability to become seeds ourselves helping others to grow and accept the knowledge and love and grace of Christ.

Your destiny in part, as a Christian is to be the seed.

The great thing about the seed is that it has everything inside of it necessary to become the plant it is intended to be, the storm helps it grow, the sun helps it mature, and whatever it is transformed into also produces more seeds because God wants us to help cultivate and fill his garden, this is his will, that when you are converted you will strengthen your brothers and sisters. In being the seed, also consider what you are planted in, as all soil or dirt is not created equal. "I have the right to do anything," you say—but not everything is beneficial. *"I have the right to do anything"—but I will not be mastered by anything."* - 1 Corinthians 6:12

 To begin to cultivate your seed, close your eyes and answer these questions.

What type of soil am I planted in?

Am I doing things that are good and beneficial for me?

What am I doing to bring others into the knowledge and love of Christ?

In order to accomplish this, think through "head, heart, and legs" for each item.

Head - What will I need to feed my mind in order to accomplish these tasks?
Heart - How will I build up resilience to be able to maintain emotional strength?
Legs - What habits will I need to form in order to accomplish these tasks?

Prayer starter
God I thank you for making me a seed, thank you for

connecting me to you. Help me to do more to be a living testimony for you. Adorn me with your praise, that the world may glorify you through my life, I exalt your holy name, and you've got my full attention. In Jesus' name I pray, amen.

DAY...8

Grow through it

"At least there is hope for a tree: If it is cut down, it will sprout again, and its new shoots will not fail. Its roots may grow old in the ground and its stump die in the soil, yet at the scent of water it will bud and put forth shoots like a plant."
Job 14:7-9 (NIV)

"We wouldn't ask why a rose that grew from the concrete for having damaged petals, in turn, we would all celebrate its tenacity, we would all love its will to reach the sun, well, we are the roses, this is the concrete and these are my damaged petals, don't ask me why, thank God, and ask me how."
Tupac Amaru Shakur, *The Rose That Grew from Concrete*

I have heard this quote by Tupac countless times, and something what jumps out at me is that this rose followed all the rules, it was planted in soil, it was waiting patiently for its season to grow, and somebody in their infinite wisdom decided to build a sidewalk where it had been planted. If this rose could talk, the rose could've complained and murmured, about how unfair life was, or it may have been discouraged because it had followed all the rules and still ran into a road block, but the interesting thing is that this rose decided to do what we all must do—grow through it. When you encounter things that are not fair in life as you sometimes will, there's only one choice, to grow through it. No matter how hard it is, how much you want to break down, choose to grow and not to groan. You can be like that rose, damaged petals and all. God gets the glory through our scars, through the damaged petals—through someone looking on and wondering how we made it over. He gets the glory from doubters who see you occupying the position that no one thought you were qualified for, graduating, when dropping out was so much easier, raising the baby and transforming from teen parent to successful adult parent. The choice is yours. You can groan through or you can grow through it.

To continue to grow through it, close your eyes and answer these questions.

What am I learning to grow through?
When I'm frustrated, do I quit or push?
What areas in my life have I grown from in the past?
How can I help my friends grow?

In order to accomplish this, think through "head, heart, and legs" for each item.

Head - What will I need to feed my mind in order to accomplish these tasks?
Heart - How will I build up resilience to be able to maintain emotional strength?
Legs - What habits will I need to form in order to accomplish these tasks?

Prayer starter

God I thank you, because of you I know I can grow through anything. I have the power to make it through any setback and convert my barriers into hurdles and jump over them into victory. Thank you for growth and continued progress in my life, and help me to always help those around me grow, as well, in the matchless name of Jesus I pray, amen.

About the Author

Daniel Bradley is the CEO and Founder of Dreams Work, Inc. a non-profit organization focused to inform, enlighten, and expose youth to critical social issues facing their communities. Daniel has over 15 years of experience in community organizing, violence prevention, youth engagement strategies and social activism. He is an agent for societal change and lives by the creed "We must teach our children to dream with their eyes open. (espoused by the African American sociologist Dr. Harry Edwards)."

Mr. Bradley is actively involved in many programs – locally and nationally – that seek to serve under-privileged youth and families; helping improve their knowledge of how to reach the full-range of their potential. He has traveled extensively throughout the continental United States as well as to various areas of Britain and the Virgin Islands to facilitate training sessions in youth development strategies. For his passion and dedication to community activism and youth work, Daniel was recognized as a Prince George's County Social Innovation Project Top 40 under 40 recipient in 2015.

Daniel studied Urban Analysis and Community Development at Georgetown University and he is currently pursuing a bachelor of science degree in Social Science at the University of Maryland University College. In June of 2016, Mr. Bradley graduated from the Skinner Leadership Institute Master's Series for Distinguished Leaders under the leadership of Dr. Barbara Williams-Skinner.

Mr. Bradley's work to improve the circumstances of, and increase opportunities for "at-risk" young people and communities is strongly rooted in the memory of hearing his Grandmother sing these words to him as a child "If I can help somebody, as I pass along…Then my living shall not be in vain."

In addition to his thriving career in social justice, Daniel serves as a Minister under the leadership of Rev. Tony Lee at the Community of Hope A.M.E. Church in Temple Hills, Maryland.

Daniel was blessed to become a husband in November of 2015, when he married the former Shekha N. Arrington; they are looking forward to a lifetime of happiness together.

DANIEL CHRISTIAN BRADLEY
AUTHOR. ACTIVIST. PREACHER. SPIRITUAL TAILOR.

DanielChristianBradley.com